Math in F☉cus®

Singapore Math®
by Marshall Cavendish

Assessment Guide

Grade
4

Marshall Cavendish
Education

U.S. Distributor

Houghton Mifflin Harcourt.
The Learning Company™

© 2020 Marshall Cavendish Education Pte Ltd

Published by Marshall Cavendish Education
Times Centre, 1 New Industrial Road, Singapore 536196
Customer Service Hotline: (65) 6213 9688
US Office Tel: (1-914) 332 8888 | Fax: (1-914) 332 8882
E-mail: cs@mceducation.com
Website: www.mceducation.com

Distributed by
Houghton Mifflin Harcourt
125 High Street
Boston, MA 02110
Tel: 617-351-5000
Website: www.hmhco.com/programs/math-in-focus

First published 2020

ISBN 978-0-358-10320-2

Printed in China

2 3 4 5 6 7 8   1401   25 24 23 22 21 20
4500799757   B C D E F

Contents

BLANK

Preface

Welcome!

The assessments in **Math in Focus®** *Assessment Guide* accompany
Math in Focus® *Student Edition*. Assessment resources provide your teachers with the critical information they need to evaluate your achievement, determine the need for intervention, and to shape future instruction.

Math in Focus® *Assessment Guide* includes:

*   **Chapter Tests** — to help your teachers determine whether you have acquired specific skills and concepts
*   **Cumulative Reviews** — to help your teachers form a larger picture of your ongoing progress

Assessments in **Math in Focus®** *Assessment Guide* employ a variety of test item formats, including multiple-choice; short answer; and constructed response.

Today, you will take a test to show what you have learned. The test has three sections: A, B, and C. You may not use a calculator for this test. You must complete all the three sections within the allotted time.

Directions

1. Read each question and follow the directions.
2. Darken the circle next to your answer. Fill the circle completely.
   Do not make marks outside a circle.
3. Erase your mark completely if you need to change an answer.
4. Some questions ask you to show or explain your work to earn points.
5. Skip questions if you do not know the answers.
6. Review your work if you finish early.

Directions for Using an Answer Grid

1. Write your answer in the boxes at the top of the grid.
2. Write only one number or symbol in each box.
3. Do not skip any boxes when you write your answer.
4. Fill in the circle under each box that matches the number or symbol in the box.
5. There may be empty boxes left after you write your answer.
   Leave the circles under these boxes blank.
6. Look at the following examples on how to complete an answer grid.

The answer grid shows the answer 108.

The answer grid shows the answer .25.

© 2020 Marshall Cavendish Education Pte Ltd

Name: _____ Date: _____

Chapter Test

1

Assessment Guide
Working with Whole Numbers

Section A   Multiple-Choice Questions

1 Read the numbers.

89,724   89,427   89,247   92,478

Which is the least?

(A) 92,478

(B) 89,724

(C) 89,427

(D) 89,247

2 What is 273,629 when rounded to the nearest thousand?

(A) 273,000

(B) 273,600

(C) 273,630

(D) 274,000

3 What are the missing numbers?

60,702 = _____ + 700 + _____

(A) 6,000 and 2

(B) 6,000 and 20

(C) 60,000 and 2

(D) 60,000 and 20

4 Look for a pattern. What is the missing number?

26,783   25,783   24,783   23,783   _____

(A) 21,783

(B) 22,783

(C) 23,683

(D) 23,883

5 What is the sum of the value of 4 in 549,763 and the value of 9 in 387,962?

(A) 130,000

(B) 40,900

(C) 49,000

(D) 90,400

Section B   Short Answer Questions

6   204,803 + 50,716 =

Write your answer in the answer grid.

⦿	⦿	⦿	⦿	⦿	⦿
⓪	⓪	⓪	⓪	⓪	⓪
①	①	①	①	①	①
②	②	②	②	②	②
③	③	③	③	③	③
④	④	④	④	④	④
⑤	⑤	⑤	⑤	⑤	⑤
⑥	⑥	⑥	⑥	⑥	⑥
⑦	⑦	⑦	⑦	⑦	⑦
⑧	⑧	⑧	⑧	⑧	⑧
⑨	⑨	⑨	⑨	⑨	⑨

7   The cost of a television set is $1,298. The cost of a refrigerator is $2,501. About how much do both items cost in all?

Show your work and write your answer in the space below.

8 Store A earns $10,347. Store A earns $1,255 more than Store B.
How much do the two stores earn in all?

Show your work and write your answer in the space below.

9 Tyler creates a number pattern for Ana to complete. Ana writes her answer in the blank.

8 7 10 9 12 11 14 13 ___16___

Is Ana correct? Explain how you arrived at your answer.

Show your work and write your answer in the space below.

10 An amusement park had 5,985 visitors in March. There were 1,070 more visitors in March than in April. In May, there were 524 more visitors than the total number of visitors in March and April. How many visitors were there in May?

Show your work and write your answer in the space below.

Section C Constructed Response

11 Sara finds the difference between 37,519 and 25,378. She gets the answer 12,261.

- Explain Sara's mistake.
- What should the correct answer be?
- Explain how you arrived at your answer.

Write your answer and your work or explanation in the space below.

Amanda is thinking of a 5-digit number.

- The digit in the hundreds place is 7.
- The digit in the thousands place is the greatest possible digit.
- The digit in the ones place is double the digit in the ten thousands place.
- The digits in the thousands place and ones place add up to 17.
- The digits in the tens and ten thousands place add up to the digit in the hundreds place.

What number is Amanda thinking of?

Write your answer and your work or explanation in the space below.

Chapter Test

2

Assessment Guide
Multiplication and Division

Section A   Multiple-Choice Questions

1 Which of the following pairs of numbers have 6 as a common factor? Choose the **two** correct answers.

(A) 6 and 16

(B) 12 and 26

(C) 24 and 42

(D) 36 and 62

(E) 48 and 54

2 When a number is divided by 7, the quotient is 217 and the remainder is 4. What is the number?

(A) 1,523

(B) 1,519

(C) 1,547

(D) 1,491

3 What number does ☆ represent?

$3,928 \times 3 = ☆ + ☆$

(A) 5,892

(B) 7,856

(C) 6,856

(D) 6,846

4. What is the missing digit?

2,___45 × 2 = 4,690

(A) 1

(B) 2

(C) 3

(D) 4

5. Which numbers are common multiples of 3 and 8?
Choose the **two** correct answers.

(A) 12

(B) 24

(C) 32

(D) 48

(E) 56

Section B   Short Answer Questions

6   1,960 ÷ 8 =

Write your answer in the answer grid.

⊙	⊙	⊙	⊙	⊙	⊙
0	0	0	0	0	0
1	1	1	1	1	1
2	2	2	2	2	2
3	3	3	3	3	3
4	4	4	4	4	4
5	5	5	5	5	5
6	6	6	6	6	6
7	7	7	7	7	7
8	8	8	8	8	8
9	9	9	9	9	9

7   329 × 17 =

Write your answer in the answer grid.

⊙	⊙	⊙	⊙	⊙	⊙
0	0	0	0	0	0
1	1	1	1	1	1
2	2	2	2	2	2
3	3	3	3	3	3
4	4	4	4	4	4
5	5	5	5	5	5
6	6	6	6	6	6
7	7	7	7	7	7
8	8	8	8	8	8
9	9	9	9	9	9

8 There are 1,500 milliliters of water in a bottle. The amount of water in the pail is 4 times the amount of water in the bottle. How many milliliters of water are there in the pail?

Show your work and write your answer in the space below.

9 Mr. Jones has 3,250 grams of blueberries. His neighbor gives him another 2,750 grams of blueberries. He uses 5,250 grams of blueberries to make some jelly. He then divides the remaining blueberries equally among his 3 children. How many grams of blueberries does each child receive?

Show your work and write your answer in the space below.

10 Hailey goes for a jog in the park every 3 days. Ravi goes for a jog in the same park every 4 days. They met each other at the park on 1 March of a calendar year.

What are the next three dates they will meet again? Explain how you arrived at your answer.

Show your work and write your answer in the space below.

Section C   Constructed Response

11 There are 65 adults and 41 children going on a day tour. What is the least number of vans needed if each van can carry 9 passengers?

Bailey says the least number of vans needed is 11 because the quotient of 106 ÷ 9 is 11.

- Explain Bailey's mistake.
- What should the correct answer be?
- Explain how you arrived at your answer.

Write your answer and your work or explanation in the space below.

12 When a number is divided by 6, the remainder is 2.
When the same number is divided by 7, the remainder is 3.
What is the least possible number?

Daniel says that the least possible number is 38.
Is Daniel correct? Explain how you arrived at your answer.

Write your answer and your work or explanation in the space below.

Assessment Guide
Cumulative Review 1

Section A Multiple-Choice Questions

1 Read the numbers.

43,215   43,125   43,521   43,512

Which is the greatest?

(A) 43,125

(B) 43,215

(C) 43,512

(D) 43,521

2 A number, when rounded to the nearest thousand, is 577,000. What could the number be?
Choose the **three** correct answers.

(A) 575,300

(B) 576,653

(C) 576,799

(D) 577,212

(E) 577,500

(F) 580,000

3 What is 89,005 in expanded form?

(A) 8,000 + 9,000 + 5

(B) 80,000 + 9,000 + 5

(C) 80,000 + 9,000 + 50

(D) 80,000 + 90,000 + 500

4 Look for a pattern. What is the missing number?

13,789   14,789   15,789   16,789   _____

(A) 18,789

(B) 17,789

(C) 16,889

(D) 16,689

5 Look at the number 130,423. Which place is the digit 0 in?

(A) hundred thousands

(B) ten thousands

(C) thousands

(D) hundreds

6 Which equations are true?
Choose the **two** correct answers.

(A) $73 - 45 = 43 - 25$

(B) $65 - 39 = 45 - 29$

(C) $50 + 12 = 48 + 15$

(D) $47 + 25 = 50 + 22$

(E) $53 + 19 = 97 - 25$

Section B Short Answer Questions

11 $425{,}783 - 167{,}902 =$

Write your answer in the answer grid.

12 $265 \times 30 =$

Write your answer in the answer grid.

13 The population of penguins on an island is 27,000 when rounded to the nearest thousand. Find the greatest possible number of penguins.

Write your answer in the answer grid.

14 Find the common factors of 8 and 36.

Show your work and write your answer in the space below.

15 Find the fourth multiple of 7.

Show your work and write your answer in the space below.

16 Find all the prime numbers from 1 to 20. Explain how you arrived at your answers.

Show your work and write your answer in the space below.

© 2020 Marshall Cavendish Education Pte Ltd

17 Jacob thinks of a number between 20 and 30. When the number is divided by 4, it has a remainder of 3. What is the least value of the number? Explain how you arrived at your answer.

Show your work and write your answer in the space below.

18 There were 16,738 people at a basketball game. 3,241 of them were children and the rest were adults. How many more adults than children were there at the basketball game?

Show your work and write your answer in the space below.

22 The prices of two types of vases at a shop are shown below.

Small vase	$17
Large vase	$23

Ms. Smith bought an equal number of small vases and large vases. She paid $520 for all the vases. How many vases did Ms. Smith buy altogether?

Write your answer and your work or explanation in the space below.

23 A melon and a bunch of bananas cost $12. 7 melons and 5 bunches of bananas cost $74.

- How much does each melon cost?
- How much does each bunch of bananas cost?

Write your answers and your work or explanation in the space below.

Chapter Test

3

Assessment Guide
Fractions and Mixed Numbers

Section A   Multiple-Choice Questions

1 How many fourths are there in $3\frac{1}{4}$?

(A) 7

(B) 8

(C) 12

(D) 13

2 Which of the following has the same value as $\frac{2}{9} \times 18$?

(A) $\frac{9}{2} \times 18$

(B) $9 \times \frac{18}{2}$

(C) $2 \times \frac{9}{18}$

(D) $2 \times \frac{1}{9} \times 18$

3 On Monday, June worked at a bookstore for $4\frac{2}{3}$ hours. She worked $1\frac{1}{3}$ hours less on Tuesday. Which of the following expressions can be used to find the number of hours she worked on Tuesday?

(A) $4\frac{2}{3} - 1\frac{1}{3}$

(B) $4\frac{2}{3} + 1\frac{1}{3}$

(C) $\frac{2}{3} - \frac{1}{3} + 4 + 1$

(D) $\frac{2}{3} + \frac{1}{3} + 4 - 1$

4 Which pairs of fractions show a correct comparison?
Choose the **two** correct answers.

(A) $\frac{2}{3} > \frac{1}{4}$

(B) $\frac{3}{5} < \frac{3}{8}$

(C) $\frac{4}{5} > \frac{3}{4}$

(D) $\frac{3}{8} > \frac{2}{3}$

(E) $\frac{1}{10} > \frac{7}{10}$

5 There are 8 students in an art class. Each student uses $\frac{3}{4}$ of a bottle of paint. How many bottles of paint do they use in all?

(A) 24

(B) 10

(C) 8

(D) 6

Section B   Short Answer Questions

6 Express $5\frac{1}{4}$ as an improper fraction.

Show your work and write your answer in the space below.

7 What is the missing number?

$$\frac{2}{5} = \frac{}{10}$$

Write your answer in the answer grid.

8 This question has two parts.

Part A

Riley baked a chicken pie. She ate $\frac{2}{8}$ of the chicken pie.

Her sister ate $\frac{1}{8}$ of the same chicken pie. What fraction of the chicken pie did they eat in all?

Show your work and write your answer in the space below.

Part B

Riley mixed $\frac{3}{5}$ liter of orange juice and $\frac{4}{5}$ liter of pineapple juice to make some fruit punch. She wants to fill a 1-liter bottle with fruit punch. Does Riley have enough fruit punch to fill the bottle? Explain.

Show your work and write your answer in the space below.

9 Layla has some ribbons. $\frac{2}{5}$ of the ribbons are striped ribbons and the rest are polka-dotted ribbons. $\frac{7}{9}$ of the polka-dotted ribbons are blue and the rest are pink. Layla has 10 pink polka-dotted ribbons. How many ribbons does she have in all?

Show your work and write your answer in the space below.

Section C Constructed Response

10 Ms. Jones buys $1\frac{3}{8}$ kilograms of meat. She used $\frac{7}{8}$ kilogram of it to make some stew. Ms. Jones needs $\frac{5}{8}$ kilogram of meat to make burgers for a party the next day.

- How much meat does Ms. Jones have left after making the stew? Give your answer as a fraction in simplest form.
- Does Ms. Jones have enough meat to make the burgers?
- Explain how you arrived at your answer.

Write your answer and your work or explanation in the space below.

$\frac{2}{3} \times 5 =$

Ana was tasked to find the answer.

Ana said that the product of $\frac{2}{3}$ and 5 is $3\frac{1}{3}$.

- Was Ana correct?
- Explain how you arrived at your answer.

Write your answer and your work or explanation in the space below.

Assessment Guide
Decimals

Section A   Multiple-Choice Questions

1 What is the total amount of water in the containers?

(A) 2.04 L

(B) 2.4 L

(C) 20.4 L

(D) 24 L

2 Look at 65.34. Which digit is in the tenths place?

(A) 6

(B) 5

(C) 4

(D) 3

3 What is 25 dollars 5 cents in decimal form?

(A) $0.25

(B) $2.55

(C) $25.05

(D) $25.50

4 What is the missing expression?
1.09 is equal to _____.
Choose the **two** correct answers.

(A) $1 + \frac{9}{10}$

(B) $1 + \frac{9}{100}$

(C) $\frac{1}{10} + \frac{9}{100}$

(D) $\frac{10}{100} + \frac{9}{100}$

(E) $\frac{100}{100} + \frac{9}{100}$

5 A number has 2 decimal places. It is 1 when rounded to the nearest whole number. What could the number be?
Choose the **three** correct answers.

(A) 1.19

(B) 1.24

(C) 1.48

(D) 1.59

(E) 1.67

(F) 1.88

Section B   Short Answer Questions

6 Use all the digits 0, 1, 5, and 3 just once to form the greatest decimal with two decimal places. (The digit 0 cannot be in the last place of the decimal.) Explain how you arrived at your answer.

Write your answer and explanation in the space below.

7 What is the missing number?

$$\frac{3}{10} + \frac{7}{100} = \frac{}{100}$$

Write your answer in the answer grid.

8 Look for a pattern. What is the missing decimal?

7.21   7.22   7.23   7.24   _____   7.26   7.27

Write your answer in the answer grid.

⊙	⊙	⊙	⊙	⊙	⊙
⓪	⓪	⓪	⓪	⓪	⓪
①	①	①	①	①	①
②	②	②	②	②	②
③	③	③	③	③	③
④	④	④	④	④	④
⑤	⑤	⑤	⑤	⑤	⑤
⑥	⑥	⑥	⑥	⑥	⑥
⑦	⑦	⑦	⑦	⑦	⑦
⑧	⑧	⑧	⑧	⑧	⑧
⑨	⑨	⑨	⑨	⑨	⑨

9 Which letter shows the correct location of 63.8 on the number line? Explain how you arrived at your answer.

Write your answer and explanation in the space below.

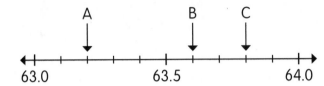

10 What is 0.32 as a fraction in simplest form?

Show your work and write your answer in the space below.

Section C   Constructed Response

11 Mr. Sanchez asked his students to guess a decimal he was thinking of. He gave them some clues.

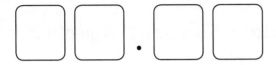

Clues:

A The digits 0, 1, and 2 are not used in the decimal.

B The digit in the hundredths place is the greatest 1-digit number that is even.

C The digit in the ones place is 1 more than the digit in the tenths place.

D The digit in the hundredths place is twice the digit in the tens place.

E The digit in the tenths place is 5.

Find the decimal.
Write your answer and your work or explanation in the space below.

12 String A is 0.6 meter long. String B is 0.21 meter long. Vijay writes a comparison for 0.6 and 0.21.

0.6 < 0.21

Vijay says that String B is longer than String A because 21 is greater than 6. Explain Vijay's mistake.

Write your answer and your work or explanation in the space below.

Name: _____ Date: _____

Assessment Guide
Cumulative Review 2

Section A   Multiple-Choice Questions

1 Which of the following is equal to $6 \times \frac{2}{3}$?
Choose the **two** correct answers.

(A) 4

(B) $\frac{24}{3}$

(C) $12 \times \frac{3}{2}$

(D) $6 \times 2 \times \frac{2}{3}$

(E) $\frac{2}{3} + \frac{2}{3} + \frac{2}{3} + \frac{2}{3} + \frac{2}{3} + \frac{2}{3}$

2 How many halves are there in $5\frac{1}{2}$?

(A) 7

(B) 8

(C) 10

(D) 11

3 What is the value of $4\frac{5}{6} - 2\frac{1}{6}$?

(A) $4\frac{1}{6}$

(B) $2\frac{5}{6}$

(C) $2\frac{1}{6}$

(D) $2\frac{2}{3}$

4 What are the missing whole numbers?

$$\boxed{} - \boxed{}\tfrac{3}{4} = 2\tfrac{1}{4}$$

(A) 4; 2

(B) 5; 2

(C) 6; 4

(D) 7; 3

5 What is the value of $1\tfrac{1}{3} + 5\tfrac{1}{3}$?

(A) $1\tfrac{2}{3}$

(B) $5\tfrac{2}{3}$

(C) $6\tfrac{1}{3}$

(D) $6\tfrac{2}{3}$

6 What is $10\tfrac{1}{5}$ as a decimal?

(A) 1.01

(B) 2.2

(C) 10.1

(D) 10.2

7 Look at 13.08. What is 0.05 less than the value of the digit in the hundredths place?

(A) 0.95

(B) 2.95

(C) 9.95

(D) 0.03

8 What is 10 dollars 8 cents in decimal form?

(A) $1.08

(B) $1.80

(C) $10.08

(D) $10.80

9 Which numbers or expressions have the same value as 163 hundredths? Choose the **two** correct answers.

(A) 0.16

(B) 1.6

(C) 1 + 0.6 + 0.03

(D) one ten six ones three tenths

(E) sixteen tenths three hundredths

10 What is 7.25 as a mixed number in simplest form?

(A) $7\frac{25}{100}$

(B) $7\frac{5}{20}$

(C) $7\frac{1}{5}$

(D) $7\frac{1}{4}$

Section B   Short Answer Questions

11 What is 0.3 less than 35.68?

Write your answer in the answer grid.

12 Use all the digits 0, 6, 3, 7, and 5 just once to form the least decimal with two decimal places. (The digit 0 cannot be in the first place of the decimal.)

Explain how you arrived at your answer.
Write your answer and explanation in the space below.

13 Look for a pattern. What is the missing decimal?

7.5   7.3   7.1   _____   6.7   6.5   6.3

Write your answer in the answer grid.

14 What is 71.55 when rounded to the nearest tenth?

Write your answer in the answer grid.

15 What is the missing number?

$$\frac{4}{12} = \frac{1}{\underline{}}$$

Write your answer in the answer grid.

16 Compare the decimals. Write < or >.

1.23 ◯ 1.3

17 There were $15\frac{1}{5}$ liters of water in a tank. Luke used $10\frac{3}{5}$ liters of water to wash the family car. He needed $4\frac{2}{5}$ liters of water to water the plants after that.

Did Luke have enough water to water the plants? Explain.

Show your work and write your answer in the space below.

18 This question has three parts.

Part A

Tiana has purple ribbon and green ribbon. She has $\frac{1}{5}$ meter of purple ribbon and $\frac{3}{5}$ meter of green ribbon. How much ribbon does Tiana have in all?

Show your work and write your answer in the space below.

Part B

Ana gives Tiana $\frac{2}{5}$ meter of blue ribbon. How much more green ribbon than blue ribbon does Tiana have?

Show your work and write your answer in the space below.

Part C

After giving Mariah $\frac{1}{5}$ meter of red ribbon, Ana has $\frac{2}{5}$ meter of red ribbon left. How much red ribbon did Ana have at first?

Show your work and write your answer in the space below.

Section C   Constructed Response

19 Carla has 0.3 meter of string. David has $\frac{15}{100}$ meter of string. David tells Carla that his string is longer because 15 is greater than 3. Explain David's mistake.

Write your answer and your work or explanation in the space below.

20. Jackson played a number game with his friends. He thought of a number and wrote down some clues.

Clues:
(A) The number is smaller than 7 and has 2 decimal places.
(B) The number becomes 7 when rounded to the nearest whole number.
(C) The digit in the tenths place is an even number.
(D) The digit in the hundredths place is the greatest 1-digit odd number.
(E) None of the digits are repeated.

What number did Jackson think of? Explain how you arrived at your answer.

Write your answer and your work or explanation in the space below.

21 A rectangle is divided into 12 equal parts. Zachary says that he has to shade 8 more parts so that $\frac{2}{3}$ of the rectangle is shaded.

				▓	
		▓			

- Explain Zachary's mistake.
- How many more parts should Zachary shade?
- Explain how you arrived at your answer.

Write your answer and your work or explanation in the space below.

Chapter 5

Assessment Guide
Conversion of Measurements

Section A   Multiple-Choice Questions

1 What is 2 feet 3 inches in inches?

(A) 15 inches

(B) 23 inches

(C) 24 inches

(D) 27 inches

2 Which comparison is correct?

(A) 2 pints = 2 cups

(B) 2 feet < 20 inches

(C) 3 yards > 8 feet

(D) 4 quarts > 2 gallons

3 What is 5 minutes in seconds?

(A) 50 seconds

(B) 60 seconds

(C) 100 seconds

(D) 300 seconds

4 Ariana has 4 pounds 3 ounces of flour. Her neighbor lends her another 2 pounds of flour. How much flour, in ounces, does Ariana have in all?

(A) 35 ounces

(B) 43 ounces

(C) 67 ounces

(D) 99 ounces

5 Ms. Smith made 8 bags. She used $\frac{7}{10}$ yard of cloth to make each bag. How much cloth, in yards, did Ms. Smith use to make all 8 bags?

(A) $2\frac{4}{5}$ yards

(B) $5\frac{3}{5}$ yards

(C) $7\frac{4}{5}$ yards

(D) $8\frac{7}{10}$ yards

Section B   Short Answer Questions

6 Express 5 cups in fluid ounces.

Show your work and write your answer in the space below.

7 Express 42 quarts 3 pints in pints.

Show your work and write your answer in the space below.

8 Express 2 kilometers 50 meters in meters.

Show your work and write your answer in the space below.

9 Taylor measures the length of two ribbons, Ribbon A and Ribbon B. The length of Ribbon A is 2 feet. The length of Ribbon B is 28 inches. Which ribbon is shorter? Explain.

Write your answer and explanation in the space below.

10 Alex bought 4 apples. Each apple weighed $\frac{1}{4}$ pound. He also bought a watermelon that weighed 3 pounds. What was the total weight of the fruit Alex bought?

Show your work and write your answer in the space below.

Section C   Constructed Response

11 Brian wanted to catch a 9:00 P.M. show at home. He left his office at 6:50 P.M.
He walked for 15 minutes to the train station.
He then spent 1 hour 5 minutes on the train before walking another
20 minutes to reach home.

Was Brian home in time to catch his show? Explain.

Write your answer and your work or explanation in the space below.

12 There are 40 pints of water in Tank A. There are 28 quarts of water in Tank B.

Kyle says that Tank A contains more water than Tank B because 40 is more than 28.

Do you agree with Kyle? Explain.

Write your answer and your work or explanation in the space below.

Chapter 6 Assessment Guide
Area and Perimeter

Section A   Multiple-Choice Questions

1 The length of a side of a square is 4 inches. What is the perimeter of the square?

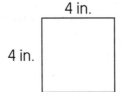

(A) 4 inches

(B) 8 inches

(C) 16 inches

(D) 36 inches

4 in.

4 in.

2 The perimeter of a rectangle is 24 meters. The length is 8 meters. What is the width of the rectangle?

(A) 4 meters

(B) 8 meters

(C) 12 meters

(D) 16 meters

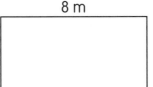

8 m

Perimeter = 24 m

3 What is the perimeter of the figure?

(A) 27 yards

(B) 39 yards

(C) 42 yards

(D) 54 yards

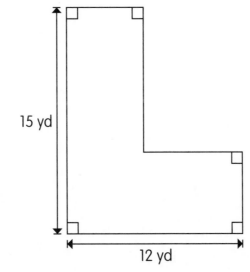

15 yd

12 yd

4 The square below is formed when the length of a rectangle is shortened by 1 mile and the width is increased by 3 miles. What is the area of the original rectangle?

Perimeter = 28 mi

(A) 4 square miles

(B) 24 square miles

(C) 32 square miles

(D) 80 square miles

5 The figure is made up of three identical squares and has a perimeter of 40 yards. What is the area of one square?

(A) 10 square yards

(B) 25 square yards

(C) 40 square yards

(D) 56 square yards

Section B   Short Answer Questions

6 Find the area of the shaded parts of the figure.

Show your work and write your answer in the space below.

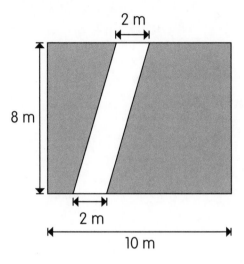

7 Michael bent a 40-inch wire into a square. What is the area inside the square?

Show your work and write your answer in the space below.

8 Find the area and perimeter of the figure.

Show your work and write your answer in the space below.

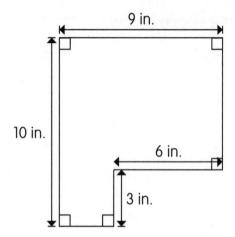

9 A rectangular pond is surrounded by a 2-meter wide lawn as shown in the diagram. Find the area of the lawn.

Show your work and write your answer in the space below.

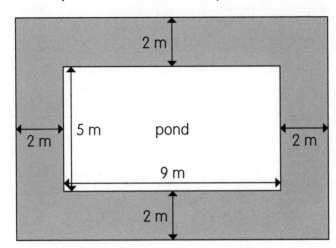

2 m

2 m   5 m   pond   2 m

9 m

2 m

10 Thomas designs a photo collage as shown below. His design is made up of a big square photo and 3 smaller square photos. The area of the collage is 192 square inches. What is length of the side of the smaller photo?

Show your work and write your answer in the space below.

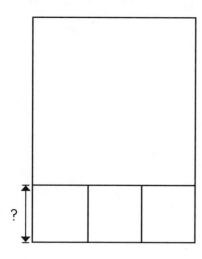

?

Section C Constructed Response

11 Sean worked out the area and perimeter of the figures below.

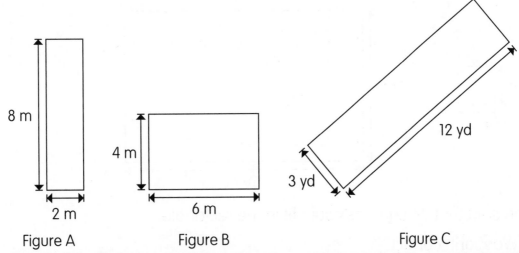

Figure A   Figure B   Figure C

Figure	Length	Width	Perimeter	Area
A	8 m	2 m	20 m	(16 m)
B	6 m	4 m	20 m	(24 cm²)
C	12 yd	3 yd	(36 yd)	(30 yd²)

Sean's mistakes are circled.

- Explain Sean's mistakes.
- What should the correct answers be?
- Explain how you arrived at your answers.

Write your answers and your work or explanation in the space below.

12 John was tasked to fit as many squares, each measuring
2 centimeters by 2 centimeters, within a rectangle measuring
12 centimeters by 8 centimeters.

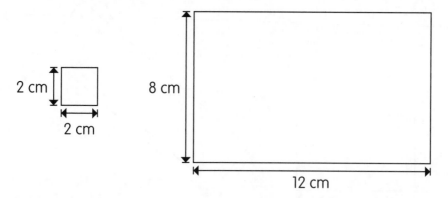

John said that 24 squares could fit in the rectangle.

- Was John correct?
- Explain how you arrived at your answer.

Write your answer and your work or explanation in the space below.

Assessment Guide
Cumulative Review 3

Section A Multiple-Choice Questions

1 What is 2 tons 500 pounds in pounds?

(A) 2,000 pounds

(B) 2,500 pounds

(C) 4,000 pounds

(D) 4,500 pounds

2 Which comparison is correct?

(A) 2 pounds < 20 ounces

(B) 2 kilometers = 2,000 meters

(C) 3 pints = 3 cups

(D) 5 quarts > 2 gallons

3 Tyler took 7 minutes to run a race. James took 467 seconds to run the same race. Who finished faster, and by how many seconds?

(A) Tyler, 47 seconds

(B) James, 47 seconds

(C) James, 100 seconds

(D) Tyler, 420 seconds

4 What is 1 yard 3 feet in feet?

(A) 3 feet

(B) 4 feet

(C) 6 feet

(D) 13 feet

5 Ms. Roberts made some fruit punch by mixing 2 quarts of apple juice, $1\frac{1}{2}$ quarts of orange juice and 3 quarts of grape juice. She served 6 quarts of the fruit punch to her guests.

Which of the following amounts represent the fruit punch **not** served to guests?
Choose the **three** correct answers.

(A) $\frac{1}{2}$ quart

(B) $\frac{1}{2}$ pint

(C) 2 cups

(D) 16 fluid ounces

(E) $\frac{1}{4}$ gallon

6 The length of a side of a square is 6 feet. What is the perimeter of the square?

(A) 6 feet

(B) 12 feet

(C) 24 feet

(D) 36 feet

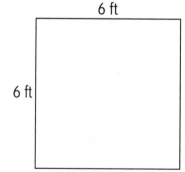

6 ft

6 ft

7 The width of a rectangle is half of its length. The width and the length of the rectangle are whole numbers greater than 2 and less than 10. What could the area of the rectangle be?
Choose the **two** possible answers.

(A) 8 square meters

(B) 16 square meters

(C) 18 square meters

(D) 32 square meters

(E) 50 square meters

8 What is the perimeter of the figure?

(A) 64 inches

(B) 60 inches

(C) 44 inches

(D) 32 inches

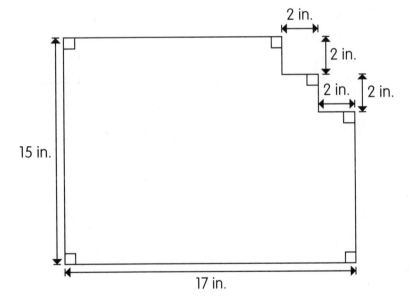

9 The perimeter of a square is 32 meters. What is its area?

(A) 16 square meters

(B) 32 square meters

(C) 64 square meters

(D) 256 square meters

Perimeter = 32 m

10 The length of a rectangle is 8 yards. The width of the rectangle is 6 yards. What is the area of the rectangle?

(A) 12 square yards

(B) 16 square yards

(C) 24 square yards

(D) 48 square yards

6 yd

8 yd

Section B   Short Answer Questions

11 Compare using <, >, or =.

55 seconds ◯ 1 minute

12 Compare using <, >, or =.

1 mile ◯ 1,700 yards

13 Express 2 yards in inches.

Show your work and write your answer in the space below.

14 Express 3 kilometers 8 meters in meters.

Show your work and write your answer in the space below.

15 Michelle has a water tank that holds 5 gallons of water. She drains out 10 pints of water. How many pints of water are left in the water tank?

Show your work and write your answer in the space below.

16 Zane bought 8 oranges and a pineapple. The weight of each orange was $\frac{1}{4}$ pound. The weight of the pineapple was 2 pounds. Find the total weight, in ounces, of the pieces of fruit Zane bought.

Show your work and write your answer in the space below.

17 Find the area of the shaded parts of the figure.

Show your work and write your answer in the space below.

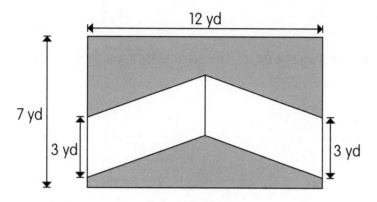

18 Find the perimeter of the figure.

Show your work and write your answer in the space below.

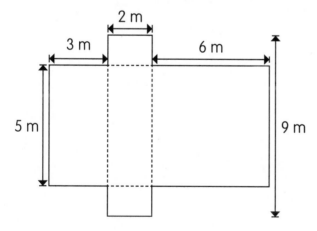

19 Chloe says the area of a square with a side length of 10 inches is larger than the area of a square with a side length of 1 foot. She says this is because 10 is greater than 1.

Explain Chloe's mistake.

Show your work and write your answer in the space below.

20 Find the area of the figure.

Show your work and write your answer in the space below.

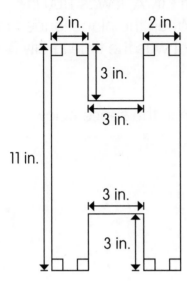

Section C   Constructed Response

21 A plane left City A for City B. When it was 1200 in City A, it was 1100 in City B. The flight was 3 hours 20 minutes long. When the plane landed in City B, the clock in the airport showed 1430. What was the time in City A when the plane departed?

Write your answer and your work or explanation in the space below.

22 Tyler had two identical rectangular pieces of paper overlapping as shown. The area of the overlapping part was 5 in². What was the area of the parts that were not overlapping?

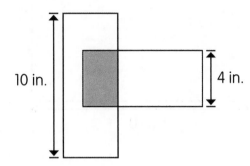

10 in. 4 in.

Write your answer and your work or explanation in the space below.

23 Ivan had to lay tiles each measuring 2 feet by 2 feet in a room. The rectangular floor of the room measured 8 yards by 5 yards.

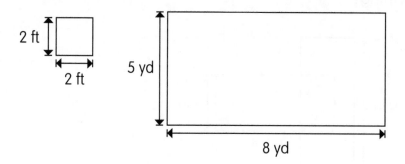

- How many tiles could fit on the floor?
- What is the area of the floor that would be left uncovered?

Write your answer and your work or explanation in the space below.

Chapter

7

Assessment Guide
Angles and
Line Segments

Section A   Multiple-Choice Questions

1 What is another way of naming ∠ACD?

(A) ∠w

(B) ∠x

(C) ∠y

(D) ∠z

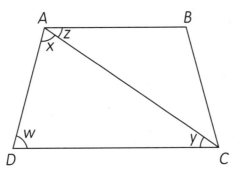

2 Is ∠r an acute angle or an obtuse angle? Without using a protractor, what is likely to be the measure of ∠r?

(A) acute angle, 13°

(B) acute angle, 73°

(C) obtuse angle, 110°

(D) obtuse angle, 155°

3 Which angle shows a $\frac{1}{2}$-turn?

(A) ∠p

(B) ∠q

(C) ∠r

(D) ∠s

4 $\angle COD$ is a straight angle. Which equation can be used to calculate $\angle p$?

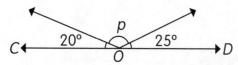

(A) $\angle p = 180° + 25° + 20°$

(B) $\angle p + 25° + 20° = 180°$

(C) $\angle p + 25° = 180° + 20°$

(D) $\angle p + 20° = 180° + 25°$

5 Which angle has a measure of 75°? Use a protractor to help you.

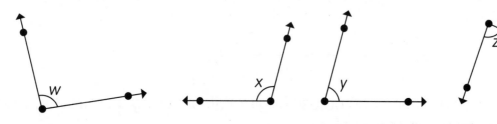

(A) $\angle w$

(B) $\angle x$

(C) $\angle y$

(D) $\angle z$

Section B Short Answer Questions

6 *PQRS* is a rectangle. Find the measure of ∠*p*.

Show your work and write your answer in the space below.

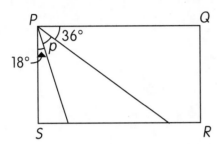

7 The measure of ∠*BOC* is 130°. Draw and label the angle.

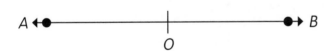

8 Draw a line segment perpendicular to the given line segment through point *A*.

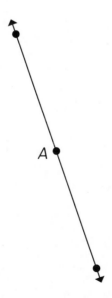

9 What are the measures of ∠r and ∠s? Use a protractor to help you.

Write each answer in the blank.

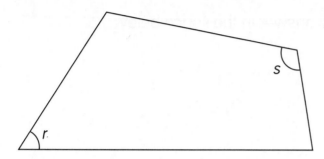

$m\angle r =$ _____

$m\angle s =$ _____

10 Draw a line segment parallel to the given line segment through point *B*.

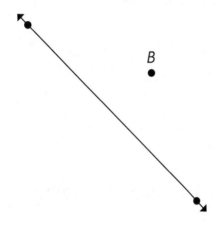

B

Section C   Constructed Response

11 Blake and John study ∠e below. Blake says that ∠e is an acute angle.
John says that ∠e is less than a straight angle.

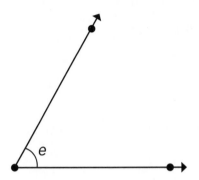

- Is Blake's statement correct?
- Is John's statement correct?
- Explain how you arrived at your answers.

Write your answers and your work or explanation in the space below.

12 Sara and Olivia study ∠AOB below. Sara says that the measure of ∠AOB is 30°. Olivia says that the measure of ∠AOB is 150°.

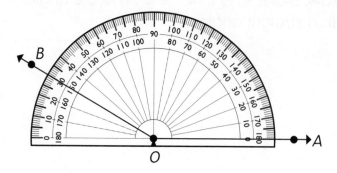

Who made a mistake? Explain.

Write your answer and your work or explanation in the space below.

Assessment Guide
Polygons and Symmetry

Chapter Test 8

Section A Multiple-Choice Questions

1 Which lines are lines of symmetry for the figure?

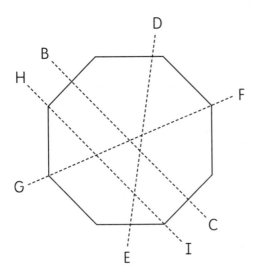

(A) *BC* and *DE*

(B) *BC* and *FG*

(C) *DE* and *HI*

(D) *DE*, *FG* and *HI*

2 Which statement about polygons is **not** correct?

(A) A rectangle has four right angles.

(B) All rhombuses are parallelograms.

(C) All triangles have three acute angles.

(D) A square is a rectangle with four equal sides.

3 Which triangle is an acute triangle? Use a protractor to help you.

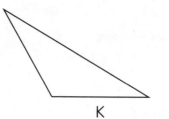 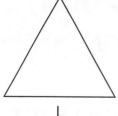 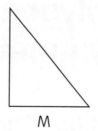 

K   L   M   N

(A) K

(B) L

(C) M

(D) N

4 Which figure is symmetric?

P   Q   R   S

(A) P

(B) Q

(C) R

(D) S

5 Which letters are not symmetric?
Choose the **two** possible answers.

(A) Y

(B) K

(C) S

(D) N

(E) M

Section B   Short Answer Questions

6 Sort the polygons into two groups. Write the letter of each polygon in the correct group.

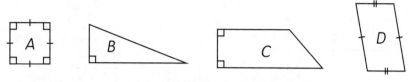

At Least One Pair of Equal Sides	No Equal Sides

7 Draw a line of symmetry for the figure.

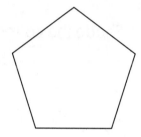

8 The figure shows half of a symmetric figure. Complete the symmetric figure with the dotted line as a line of symmetry.

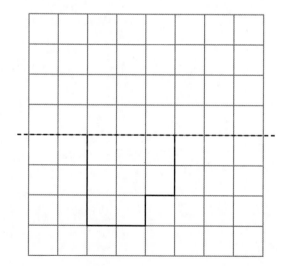

9 The figure shows half of a symmetric figure. Complete the symmetric figure with the dotted line as a line of symmetry.

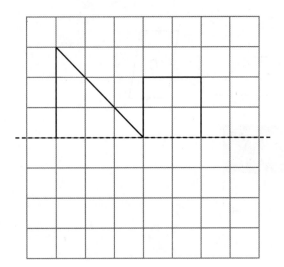

10 The dotted line in the figure below is a line of symmetry. Shade the correct squares to make a symmetric pattern.

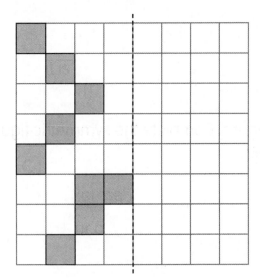

Section C   Constructed Response

11 Jason says that the shape below is a rectangle.

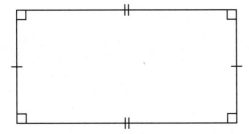

Do you agree with Jason? Explain.

Write your answer and your work or explanation in the space below.

12 Ava and Jack study the figure below. Ava says that there are only 2 lines of symmetry. Jack says that there are 4 lines of symmetry.

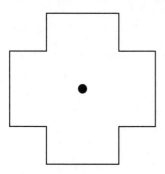

- Is Ava or Jack correct?
- Explain how you arrived at your answer.

Write your answer and your work or explanation in the space below.

Chapter Test 9

Assessment Guide
Tables and Line Graphs

Section A   Multiple-Choice Questions

1. This question has two parts.

   The line graph shows the number of cars sold in a particular week.

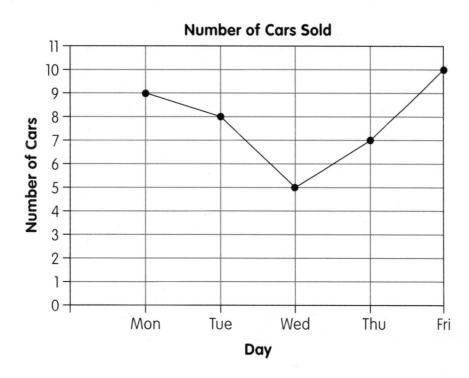

Number of Cars Sold

Part A

How many cars were sold on Thursday?

(A) 9

(B) 8

(C) 7

(D) 5

Part B

How many more cars were sold on Friday than on Tuesday?

(A) 1

(B) 2

(C) 3

(D) 5

2 This question has three parts.

The line graph shows the number of cameras sold in a particular week in a particular store.

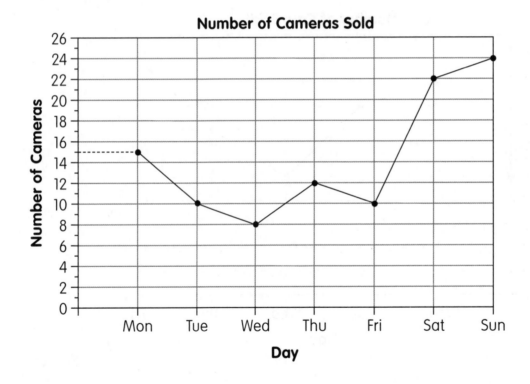

Part A

How many more cameras were sold on Thursday than on Wednesday?

(A) 2

(B) 4

(C) 7

(D) 20

Part B

On which two days were the number of cameras sold the same?

(A) Tuesday and Friday

(B) Monday and Thursday

(C) Wednesday and Friday

(D) Saturday and Sunday

Part C

Which statement about the line graph is true?

(A) The difference between the highest amount of sales and lowest amount of sales is 14 cameras.

(B) The store sold its 100th camera for the week on Saturday.

(C) 46 cameras were sold on Saturday and Sunday altogether.

(D) The number of cameras sold on Sunday is $\frac{1}{4}$ of the total number of cameras sold in the week.

Section B Short Answer Questions

3 Count the number of each type of sticker. Use tally marks to record the data.

Write your answers in the table below.

Sticker	Tally
♥	
🙂	
☁	

4 The table shows the number of medals won by different schools in a sports event. Some data is missing.

Write your answers in the table below.

School	Bronze	Silver	Gold	Total Number
A	20	25	15	60
B	12	14		40
C	15		25	55
D		8	20	
Total		62	74	200

5 The table shows information about 30 coins that Thomas, Alex, Sara, and Gavin have each.
Some data is missing.

Write your answers in the table below.

Name	Number of Quarters	Value of Quarters ($0.25)	Number of Dimes	Value of Dimes ($0.10)	Total Value
Thomas	15	$3.75	15	$1.50	$5.25
Alex	10	$2.50	20	$2.00	$4.50
Sara			12	$1.20	
Gavin	8	$2.00			

6 This question has two parts.
The table shows the number of visitors to an amusement park over six months.

Month	January	February	March	April	May	June
Number of Visitors	2,200	2,000	2,500	2,400	2,000	2,800

Part A

How many visitors were there in May?

Write your answer in the answer grid.

Part B

How many fewer visitors were there in January than in June?

Show your work and write your answer in the space below.

Section C Constructed Response

7 The line graph shows the height of a bean plant over a five-week period.

Height of Bean Plant over Five Weeks

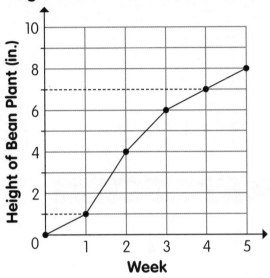

- In which week was the height of the bean plant 7 inches?
- From the graph, Leah said that the greatest increase in the height of the bean plant was between weeks 1 and 2. Is Leah correct? Explain.

Write your answer and your work or explanation in the space below.

8 Alex counted the number of each type of shape. He presented the data in a table.

Shape	Tally	Number of Shapes
△ Triangle	//	2
▢ Square	ՄՄ I	6
◯ Circle	////	4

Did Alex present the data correctly? Explain.

Write your answer and your work or explanation in the space below.

Assessment Guide
Cumulative Review 4

Section A Multiple-Choice Questions

1 Is ∠s an acute angle or an obtuse angle?
Without using a protractor, what is likely to be the
measure of ∠s?

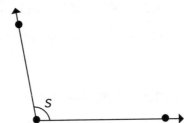

  (**A**) acute angle, 48°

  (**B**) acute angle, 88°

  (**C**) obtuse angle, 100°

  (**D**) obtuse angle, 160°

2 Which statement about turns and angle measures is true?

  (**A**) A $\frac{1}{4}$-turn is 90 right angles.

  (**B**) A straight angle is the same as a $\frac{1}{2}$-turn.

  (**C**) An angle that turns through $\frac{3}{4}$ of a full turn has a measure of 180°.

  (**D**) An angle that turns through $\frac{1}{360}$ of a full turn has a measure of 360°.

3 What fraction of a turn is 270°?

  (**A**) $\frac{1}{2}$

  (**B**) $\frac{1}{4}$

  (**C**) $\frac{1}{8}$

  (**D**) $\frac{3}{4}$

4 Caroline sorted some polygons into two groups as shown.

X	Y
Rhombus	Right triangle
Obtuse triangle	Rectangle
Parallelogram	Square

What do **X** and **Y** represent?

(A) X: At least one pair of parallel sides; Y: No parallel sides

(B) X: No parallel sides; Y: At least one pair of parallel sides

(C) X: No right angles; Y: At least one right angle

(D) X: Symmetric shapes; Y: Non-symmetric shapes

5 Which figure has a line of symmetry?

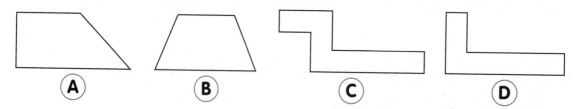

(A)   (B)   (C)   (D)

6 A paper was folded and a figure was cut out as shown.

How will the figure look when the paper is unfolded?

(A)

(B)

(C)

(D)

7 This question has two parts.
The line graph shows the number of visitors to a museum in a particular week.

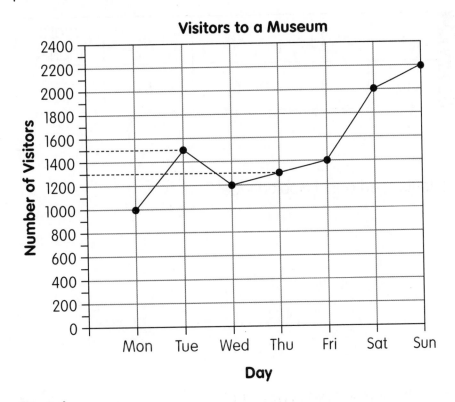

Visitors to a Museum

Part A

How many visitors were there on Tuesday?

(A) 1,300

(B) 1,400

(C) 1,500

(D) 1,600

Part B

On which day were there 700 fewer visitors than on Saturday?

(A) Monday

(B) Wednesday

(C) Thursday

(D) Friday

8 This question has two parts.

The table shows the number of books that students in a class read in a week.

Number of Books Read	1	2	3	4	more than 4
Number of Students	10	8	6	5	10

Part A

How many students read only 1 book a week?

(A) 5

(B) 6

(C) 8

(D) 10

Part B

Which statement about the table is **not** true?

(A) 15 students read more than 3 books in a week.

(B) The total number of books read in a week was 39.

(C) 18 students read 2 books or less in a week.

(D) Less than half the class read 4 books or more.

Section B Short Answer Questions

9 The measure of ∠QOR is 115°. Draw and label the angle.

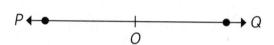

10 What are the measures of ∠w and ∠x? Use a protractor to help you.

Write each answer in the blank.

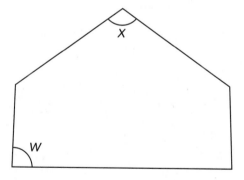

$m\angle w =$ _____

$m\angle x =$ _____

11 Shanti has a square piece of paper. She wants to cut the paper as shown. What is the measure of ∠x?

Show your work and write your answer in the space below.

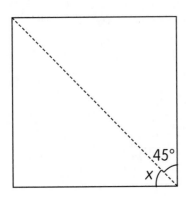

12 Draw a line segment parallel to the given line segment through point B.

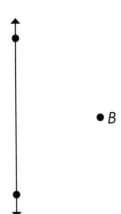

13 Draw a line segment perpendicular to the given line segment through point *A*.

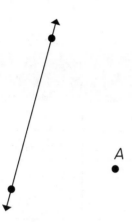

A

14 The dotted line in the figure below is a line of symmetry. Shade the correct squares to make a symmetric pattern.

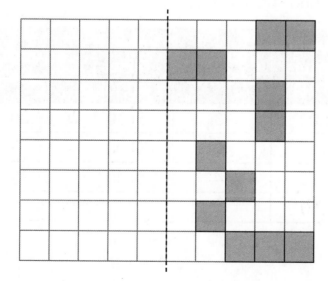

15 The table shows the number of waffles sold by 4 children in a fundraising event. Some data is missing.

Write your answers in the table below.

Name	Vanilla Waffles	Chocolate Waffles	Strawberry Waffles	Total Number
Alex	8		13	36
Ella	12	14	14	40
June		6	12	
Noah		8		35
Total	59	43		150

16 The table shows information about 25 coins that Caleb, John, Alyssa, and Faith have each. Some data is missing.
John says that he has the greatest amount of money while Faith has the least. Is John correct? Explain.

Write your answers in the table and space below.

Name	Number of Quarters	Value of Quarters ($0.25)	Number of Dimes	Value of Dimes ($0.10)	Total Value
Caleb	12	$3.00	13	$1.30	$4.30
John			10	$1.00	
Alyssa	11	$2.75	14	$1.40	$4.15
Faith	6	$1.50			

17 Draw a line of symmetry for the letter.

18 The table below shows the number of movie tickets sold at a movie theater over six days.

Day	1	2	3	4	5	6
Number of Tickets Sold	3,506	4,250	2,753	5,255	4,002	3,758

How many more tickets were sold on day 2 than on day 5?

Write your answer in the answer grid.

Section C   Constructed Response

19 Michael is looking at the letters in the names below.

Michael says that each letter in the name, AVA, has one line of symmetry. He says that one of the letters in the name, IAN, has more than one line of symmetry, but one of them does not have any.

- Is everything that Michael has said correct?
- Explain how you arrived at your answer.

Write your answer and your work or explanation in the space below.

20 The table shows Diego's mass over the last six years.

Age (years)	0	1	2	3	4	5	6
Mass (kg)	3	9	11	14	18	21	25

Eric says that he wants to present the data in a bar graph.

- Is Eric's choice of graph suitable? If his choice is not suitable, which type of graph should he use?
- Explain how you arrived at your answer.

Write your answer and your work or explanation in the space below.

21 The line graph below shows the amount of water used by the Smiths each week, over five weeks.

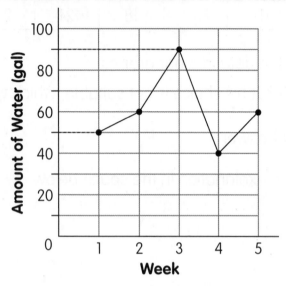

Amount of Water Used over Five Weeks

- During which week did the Smiths use the least amount of water?
- From the graph, Amy tells her father that the greatest increase in water usage was between weeks 2 and 3. Is Amy correct? Explain.

Write your answers and your work or explanation in the space below.